Lazy Habits - The Pragmatic Guide To Create Powerful Habits

Laurent Meri

Published by LAURENT MERI, 2023.

Table of Contents

For the dreamers who weave the tapestry of future realities with the threads of imagination, and for the fighters who valiantly strive to create a world as beautiful as the dreams they are born from

Wanna Hear a Little Secret? Keep It Short

In today's world of super-short attention spans, you gotta trim the fat if you want to pay attention to hot takes. Sure, jumbo books look impressive on your shelf. But when it comes to real talk, shorter is sweeter.

Short books give you a laser-focused highlight without all the boring backstory or fluff. Their every sentence packs a punch, not wasted words.

Got an earth-shattering idea? Don't bury it under 600 pages of dust-dry prose. Distil that sucker down to its purest, minimalist form. Like a perfectly blended smoothie, filter out the unnecessary chunks for maximum impact.

Besides, who has time for lengthy door topper tomes anymore? We want knowledge in bite-size nuggets now. With fit-for-purpose books, you can suck down those nourishing morsels in a few sittings, retaining way more. Really let the savoury flavours marinate.

And don't forget the sharing! Itty bitty ideas spread like hot fire because everyone has time for a quick but amazing story. Just ask that monk dude with the Ferrari - his cliff's notes wisdom went viral faster than a Kanye rant.

So do yourself a favour and keep it short. Chop off any unnecessary padding. Get straight to the good stuff and deliver it with gravitas.

Less is more when you choose each word with care.

A Note Before We Begin...

First, thank you sincerely for reading this book! My goal is providing value and helping upgrade people's lives through habit changes.

If you find this guide useful, you'd be doing me a massive favour by taking a minute to leave an honest positive review on the platform you bought the book from. Here's why it matters:

Positive word-of-mouth is crucial for indie books to spread and make an impact. Your review gives the algorithms a signal that this info is changing lives.

That then allows me to reach and help many more people just like you. My dream is improving lives at scale through tiny habit shifts!

But that can't happen without reviews from awesome readers. And you are an AWE...SOMe reader. So if you're feeling this book, please boost the signal with a positive review. It would mean the world to me and this community.

Changing ingrained human habits is hard – we need all the help we can get! With your small action, together we can compound this message and create transformations.

Plus, you'll likely inspire someone in your life who needs this book too. Paying it forward creates ripples.

Okay, sincerely thank you for even considering leaving your feedback. Now let's dive into these unbelievable habit upgrades!

Introduction

What's good my friends! Welcome to the book that's here to make habit change stupid easy. For real - no more lame tips about grit and willpower. We're taking the laid-back lazy person's path to awesomeness.

See, the problem with most self-help junk is it preaches hardcore discipline from day one. Sweat at 5am daily! Meal prep kale salads weekly! Manifest your dreams through visualisation rituals!

Yeah right. That regimental mindset works for like 1% of crazy motivated robots. But for us normal folks, that military grind leads nowhere.

Even with the best intentions, we end up burnt out and back to binge-watching Netflix every time. Ugh!

What we need is the art of sneaky habits. Micro-changes that trick our brains into self-improvement little by little on autopilot.

I call it the Jedi mind trick approach. Tiny nudges in the right direction through psychology, not sheer effort.

By the end, you'll have built killer habits - yet feel like you barely did anything! Now that's the lazy person's dream.

This book reveals the 4-rule formula for achieving greatness through micro-actions, smart sequencing, social accountability, and the magic of compound interest.

Here's what we'll cover:

First, we make habits microscopically small. I'm talking one push-up or one minute reading to start.

Tiny habits bypass our brains' resistance to change. And they stack up way faster than you expect thanks to the power of compounding.

Then, we domino stack those mini habits for momentum. Chain them together strategically so each one triggers the next automatically.

This forms effortless habit cascades like clockwork. Suddenly, you're crushing your mornings without friction.

We also leverage peer pressure to our advantage. Tell your friends about your habits for motivation. Join groups to build community. A little competition goes a long way!

Finally, we use the black magic of compound interest. Stick with micro habits consistently, and your results grow exponentially over time.

Tiny interest payments turn into massive investment gains. Posting blog posts leads to thousands of readers. Mini habit reps transform your physique and skills.

This formula allows you to steer your days through little nudges, not grand makeovers. Tiny habits build the momentum, sequencing gives flow, social pressure sustains motivation, and compounding works behind the scenes.

Before you know it, you've tricked your brain into building an awesome lifestyle through small, smart, lazy actions over time.

This book reveals the laid-back path to success. How to utilise psychology and scaled consistency to achieve greatness the easy way. I got you!

Through micro steps and milestones, you'll gain confidence and momentum and slowly transform into the person you want to be.

So get pumped! Ditch the exhausting self-help tactics and embrace the art of sneaky habits. You're about to level up your life big time with minimal effort through the 4 rule formula. Let's start!

Chapter 1: Tiny Habits - "Forget Big Goals. How Habit Microsteps Lead to Macro Success"

Friends, Dream Big But Start Small - Like, Microscopic

We all have big goals, right? Get shredded like the Rock. Write the next Harry Potter. Learn to shred like Eddie Van Halen. Travel the world in a decked out camper van.

Chasing big dreams is freakin' essential! But trying to reach those goals through massive overnight changes is a recipe for disaster.

Our lazy brains HATE discomfort and hard work. So even though you get all fired up imagining that final vision, your motivation crashes faster than a failed New Year's diet. Ugh.

When you think about the effort needed to actually reach those goals, your lizard brain is like "Hard pass, my friend! We're just gonna stay on the couch where it's safe and comfy."

So your ambitions turn into Netflix binges, and dreams gather dust like that guitar in the closet. We've all been there!

But what if I told you there's a sneaky secret strategy to trick your brain into achieving greatness? You with me? It's called...(drumroll please)...TINY HABITS!

I know, anticlimactic name for such a powerhouse concept. Let me break this baby down...

Tiny habits are exactly what they sound like - habits so laughably small and easy, you can't help but do them. We're talking one pushup, one minute of meditation, one sentence written in your novel draft.

These micro habits take zero motivation or discipline since they require barely any effort. But consistency works its magic and those tiny steps stack up over time.

After a year, you'll have done over 300 pushups without even noticing! Your meditation practice expands to hours without ever overwhelming you. And your book is writing itself sentence by sentence. Pretty sweet right?

Tiny Habits Hack Your Brain's Lazy Logic

Alright, this is the part where I let you in on the mind hacks that make tiny habits so dang effective. Your brain may be a hater, but it ain't too bright! Outsmarting it is stupid easy once you know its logic loops. Let me explain...

The genius of laughably small habits is that they fly under your brain's radar. There's no red alert resistance like with big intimidating goals.

Think about it - if I was like "Yo! Commit right now to a hardcore hour of meditation at 5am daily!" you'd shut down faster than a Windows 95 computer. Too much effort!

Your lazy lizard brain would start rationalising excuses immediately: "Uh, I'm not a morning person...I'll never wake up that early...I can't sit still for a whole hour..."

Massive goal = massive demotivation. Your brain nopes out instantly.

But suggest just ONE itty bitty minute of meditation? Your brain reacts totally differently: "Hmm, alright I guess one measly minute doesn't sound too painful. I can endure anything for 60 seconds! Sure, whatever, let's do this."

No big effort detected = no resistance activated. Bingo! Tiny habits slip under the radar.

It's like distracting a velociraptor with a laser pointer - their tiny pea brains get confused for a sec and you sprint to safety. Tiny habits confuse your inner laziness!

By the time your brain realises you've started a habit, it's too late - you already did a pushup, finished meditating, and read a sentence. Boom! Micro habit achieved!

This momentum effect builds confidence fast too. When you finish a tiny habit, your brain thinks "Oh, guess this self-improvement stuff isn't so hard after all!" Quick micro wins get it on your side.

Suddenly, things seem possible that once felt intimidating. "If I can meditate for one minute, maybe I can sit for 5 minutes consistently." Small victories lead to bigger ones.

It's like tricking a toddler into eating veggies - disguise it, make it fun, get it in their mouth before they notice! Next thing you know, they're asking for more broccoli. Tiny habits disguise themselves as easy fun.

So in summary, laughably small habits sidestep resistance, build consistency through micro wins, and compound into results that gain your brain's cooperation over time. All by sneaking up on laziness!

Again, it seems ridiculous...until it works. If you had told me I'd run 5 miles daily by starting with just 1 block a day, I'd call you crazy. But it compounds!

Outsmart your inner sloth with these micro mind hacks, and you'll be shocked at the changes you can trick yourself into. Tiny habits help you negotiate with your resistance rather than fighting it directly. Give laziness an inch, it takes a mile!

Tiny Habits Stealthily Stack Up Under Your Brain's Radar

Alright, the next mind hack that makes tiny habits so powerful is the way they sneakily stack up results through the magic of compounding interest. This is how tiny changes transform into titanic improvement down the road.

Here's the thing - if I was like "You gotta write one page of your book every single day this year to finish it!" That sounds intimidating upfront. 365 pages is a big goal.

Your brain would be sceptical and resistant from day one. But propose just writing one teensy page per day? No problem, your brain thinks.

"Pshh, one measly page? That's like 5 min of effort. Yeah I guess I can muster up that much motivation." No resistance detected.

But then, through the power of consistency and compounding, those tiny sentences turn into full pages, which turn into chapters, which turn into books!

It stacks up completely under your lazy brain's radar. After a year, you'll have a 365 page manuscript, yet the habit always stayed at one page so your brain never fretted. Pretty slick huh?

It's the same with meditation. One minute a day seems totally harmless. But after a decade you'll have meditated for over 60 hours! Your habit stayed small, but the time compounded.

This stealth stacking works for any habit. One pushup leads to 365 reps in a year. One minute guitar practice leads to hours of playing. Tiny input, huge output!

That's the magic of compounding! Your brain just sees quick little micro habits each day, no struggle. But the results accumulate into massive change before you even realize it.

It's like a magic show misdirection - the tiny habits keep your brain's attention while the compounding happens somewhere else. Poof! Suddenly you know guitar. Amazing!

Oogway's Wisdom

This concept reminds me of one of my favourite wisdom nuggets from the movie Kung Fu Panda:

"One often meets his destiny on the road he takes to avoid it."

At first, you're just trying to build an easily manageable habit. But those micro habits ultimately stack up into your destiny - a black belt, novel, business, whatever goal!

The tiny habits just keep your scepticism at bay long enough for compounding to work its magic. Once you have amazing results, your brain stops resisting.

Laughably small habits let you fly under the radar at first. Their stealthy stacking effect leads to unbelievable transformation before your brain can fret.

It's like accidentally discovering a hidden ancient tomb after absentmindedly kicking a small stone everyday. Tiny input, huge output!

Embrace the 1% Rule to Let Tiny Habits Work Their Magic

Alright, at this point you may be wondering how freakin' tiny you should go when starting these micro habits. Let me end the guesswork for you.

I recommend using the 1% rule - make your beginning habit just 1% of the bigger goal you want to eventually achieve. It keeps things stupidly small while still moving you incrementally towards greatness.

Let's use some examples:

Want to eventually do 100 pushups? Start with just a single rep. 1 pushup is 1% of 100. It's as tiny as it gets!

But it starts building consistency in the exercise habit without overwhelming you. Once that's solid, go to 2 pushups, then 5, and so on.

Want to run 5 miles daily someday? Begin by running just 1 single block. We're talking like 500 steps. This tiny habit is achievable even when you're exhausted and unmotivated.

Again, it gets you steadily rucking without burning out fast like trying to suddenly run for miles. Stick with 1 block, then go to 2 blocks once that's automatic. Slowly build up over weeks, months and years.

Want to learn guitar? On day one, just practise holding the instrument and plucking a single string. Do it for just 60 seconds. That's your 1% habit to start ingraining consistency.

It avoids paralysing thoughts of having to master complex chords and songs right away. Once 1 minute feels easy, go for 2. Then 5. The habit stacks up.

You get the idea right? Start with an almost stupidly easy micro habit that even Mindless Me on my worst day can handle.

Remove all possible friction and excuses so you stick to it. Tiny habits need to be frog-in-a-pot water levels gradual at first.

And what about the power of Incremental progress

Here's why this works so well: incremental progress builds momentum and consistency faster than sporadic intense effort.

Doing one pushup every day for a year will make you exponentially stronger than doing 100 pushups once a month. Even though technically the volume is the same.

Daily practice - even tiny - builds the habit, muscle memory, and consistency. Sporadic efforts never last despite bigger volume per session.

So embrace those 1% steps! Keep your habits tiny but utterly consistent. This incremental progress trains your brain and body for the long haul.

Patience and Micro Wins

This does require patience. One pushup won't make anyone jacked. But after 6 months, you'll suddenly notice serious gains you never expected.

Get just 1% better through micro habits, and your baseline rises every day. The improvements compound under the radar. Consistency rules all.

Remember the wise saying: "Inch by inch, life's a cinch. Yard by yard, life is hard." Take it inch by inch! Tiny habits for the win.

With micro changes, you also get frequent quick wins which build motivation. Your brain goes "Hey, I DID actually get better today!" versus struggling hard with no obvious progress.

So in summary, the 1% rule creates habits tiny enough for automatic consistency, incremental gains that drive real change, and quick wins that boost morale for the long journey.

It may feel silly at first. But trust in the process and the power of tiny habits. They work absolute wonders over time through stealthy stacking and consistency.

Just keep that first habit jump laughably small using the 1% rule. Remove any chance of friction. Consistency first, intensity later.

Warren Buffet started with 1%

Warren Buffett is the perfect example of how embracing tiny steps leads to incredible outcomes over a lifetime.

One of the richest men in the world, Buffett accumulated his vast fortune not through risky get-rich-quick schemes, but by incrementally investing in strong companies for the long-term.

When Warren first started out, he didn't rush to invest millions at once. He began by diligently researching companies and making small, 1% investments as opportunities arose.

Over decades, these tiny gains compounded year after year, like snowballs rolling down a hill, gathering size and momentum. Small became big.

In the 1960s, Warren slowly invested in Coca-Cola stock, gradually accumulating a massive position over 30+ years. He started small, stayed consistent, and allowed compounding to work its magic.

Now his Coke stock is worth billions, even though he originally only invested thousands. Tiny habits and incremental gains created his wealth.

He did the same for his investment in Bank Of America and Apple corporation, today it seems obvious but then it seemed small... tiny

Warren Buffett is the epitome of stealthy stacking and the tortoise mindset. He embodies the power of starting with tiny habits, pursued consistently over time.

Like the old tortoise and hare fable, Warren's slow and steady approach beat the speculation of hasty investors looking for quick wins. Patience pays off.

So follow Warren's example. Resist the urge to rush into big changes. Start small, stay consistent, keep improving 1% at a time. Your habits will compound into something great over the long run.

How Tiny Habits Transform Your Mindset And Identity

Alright folks, here's something huge to realise - tiny habits don't just change your skills and physique over time. They actually transform your entire mindset and confidence too.

When you first start with these micro habits, you may feel silly. One pushup a day - how's that gonna make me the next Rock? Seems pointless.

But when you stick with it, suddenly your self-image starts to shift. After a month you realise - hey, I did actually stick to this habit consistently. I followed through.

This transforms how you view yourself. You start adopting a new identity of someone who shows up. A doer, not just a dreamer. You LEVELLED UP!

The confidence and momentum snowballs from there. Soon you increase to two pushups, then five, then ten. After a year, you can do way more than you ever imagined when starting with one.

But the physical strength isn't even the biggest change. What developed in the process was discipline, consistency, belief in yourself. Your mindset grew stronger.

This is massive because most people try to change from the outside first - just focus on getting into shape or learning some skill.

But tiny habits work from the INSIDE OUT. Your inner confidence and identity grow through proving to yourself that you can show up each day.

This gradually transforms who you are at your core. And from that place of discipline, external changes come MUCH easier.

You've watered the roots. The visible plant flourishes naturally.

Greats Became Greater Through Tiny Steps

The masters all know this. Michael Jordan didn't become the GOAT through a few intense weeks of practice.

Nope, it took years of consistency - starting from the basics as a kid, mastering fundamentals, gaining confidence through incremental skill gains. Brick by brick.

Yo-Yo Ma, greatest cellist alive, same thing - endless small steps over decades to refine his craft. Not sporadic crunches.

A green belt knows 50 moves practised 1000 times each. A black belt knows 1000 moves practised 50 times each. Mastery requires repetition.

So listen to the experts. Ditch the quick fix mindset. Take pride in those small habit gains - they are rewiring your mind even more than your body.

It's Levelling Up!

Treat the journey like a video game. Each micro habit completed is like gaining an XP point, a badge, levelling up.

Celebrate the tiny wins. Progress takes time, but bank every small step forward.

Before you know it, you'll have unlocked the next stage of your quest through accumulated micro-wins. It all adds up!

Tiny habits transform you holistically over time - not just your skills or strength scores. They upgrade your underlying identity, self-image and confidence.

Stick with those mini habits and watch yourself evolve. But remember, it starts from the inside out. A black belt is a state of mind. Face yourself first.

If You Should Remember One Thing From This Chapter

Alright friends, let's recap what we learned in this chapter before moving on

First and foremost - start freakin' tiny! Like microscopic. Your lazy brain resists big changes, so keep that first habit laughably small.

Tiny habits bypass resistance, build consistency, and still compound into huge results over time. It's like a cheat code!

Remember the 1% rule - make your starting habit just 1% of the bigger goal. One pushup, one minute reading, one block running. Keep it almost embarrassingly easy.

Micro habits provide little quick wins that motivate you more than some far-off ambitious dream. Short term reward activation!

These small wins also change your identity fast. Tiny consistency builds genuine confidence and self-discipline.

Stick with those baby steps day after day, and your skills and physique transform before you know it. Consistency compounds!

Approach habit change like a video game - celebrate each tiny level up. Don't get overwhelmed by the end goal.

Alright, now that we've got the basics of tiny habits down, let's move on to chaining these small routines together for momentum...

But don't forget - start micro, build consistency through small wins, progress compounds over time. Tiny habits kickstart the magic!

Chapter 2: Big Results - "Habit Stacking: Master the Domino Effect to Effortlessly Build Momentum"

Friends, Let's Stack Habits Like Legos

Alright squad, time to take our tiny habits to the next level! In the last chapter we learned to start micro. Now we chain those munchkin habits together like freakin' Legos.

Introducing the beast that is habit stacking! Here's the deal - stack multiple mini habits back-to-back to build insane momentum. Each one triggers the next like dominos, creating an automatic routine cascade.

Once you string your habits together fluidly like Mom's pearls, motivation becomes a non-issue. The habit of trains doesn't stop, baby!

Let me paint a picture...

Imagine your ideal morning flow:

- 7:30am: Alarm goes off. You hydrate with a refreshing beverage.

- 7:32am: Energised from your drink, you bust out 1 pushup.

- 7:33am: Blood pumping, you meditate for 1 minute.

- 7:34am: Meditation primes your focus for reading 1 page.

- 7:35am: Reading gives you an insight to journal about.

See how each habit cues the next? You move seamlessly from one routine to the next like a squirrel hopping between trees.

Once you get that habit momentum flowing, your productivity goes through the roof! It's momentum baby! No friction or motivation required.

Visualise Your Habits Like Epic Domino Ramps

Alright, now that we've got our tiny habits dialled in, let's talk about chaining them together for maximum momentum. This is where the magic really starts!

Here's what we gotta do - visualise setting up dominoes in a smart sequence, each habit knocking into the next. Keep that mental image firm.

Picture your morning routine like an elaborate domino course winding down stairs, through hallways, all interconnected. One tile tip, cascades trigger!

That first domino is your alarm clock - which then knocks down your hydration habit - which triggers you to change into workout clothes - which cues up your actual workout - which finishes with protein drink recovery. BOOM!

Each habit is constructed intentionally to cue off the previous one and flow seamlessly together. This builds momentum fast.

No friction, no hesitation, no motivation needed. Just one habit automatically triggers the next because your routine is dialled.

It's like connecting train carts before leaving the station - you hop aboard for the ride and the engine takes you effortlessly. Destination Domination!

This chaining effect works for any life area: health, productivity, personal growth, learning, creativity. Whatever the goal.

Turn Those Tiny Habits Into a Fully-Auto Rube Goldberg Machine

A well-designed habit sequence is like a Rube Goldberg machine. You kick off one simple action, and an elaborate chain reaction happens.

Suddenly you're crushing your entire morning flow with ease, no time wasted. You transition from that first domino straight into optimised productivity beast mode!

Again, the key is planning pairs that cue each other:

- After morning coffee, meditate for focus

- After meditating, change into workout clothes to spark exercise

- After exercising, drink a smoothie to refuel

The actions flow together. No effort or discipline required - just let the domino chain guide you once set up.

This works for evening routines too:

- After dinner, floss and brush teeth

- After brushing, read for leisure

- After reading, do a 5 minute reflection in your journal

- After journaling, get ready for bed

Build flowing sequences customised to your lifestyle. Experiment to find ones that fit your natural rhythms and needs.

But keep that visual of elaborate habit dominos all connecting. This mental blueprint helps it click subconsciously.

Piggyback On Existing Habit Routines For Free Momentum

Here's another sneaky hack for building killer habit momentum: piggyback new habits onto existing routines you already do without thinking.

The beauty is you skip past the hard part of establishing a new routine from scratch. Instead, leverage old rituals you're locked into for free!

Like my boy Thibault. Every morning he starts his day with juice - never skips it. So he decided to stack his new pushup habit right after pouring his OJ.

After juicing, Thibault immediately drops down and bangs out 10 pushups before anything else in his morning. Then he repeats daily.

Over time, he increased the pushup reps, but kept them chained onto his non-negotiable juice routine. After a year, he was doing 100 pushups - but it never felt hard!

See how it works? His unbreakable juice habit created automatic momentum for consistently doing pushups. The new behaviour just piggybacked on old ones.

Thibault's brain started craving the pushups as part of his morning ritual, since they were glued to his sacrosanct juice habit. No motivation needed!

This method lets you gradually increase any habit's intensity without losing steam. It stays anchored to existing momentum rituals.

What routines can you piggyback onto?

Now take a look at your regular routines - what daily habits do you already do on complete autopilot? Things like:

- Morning coffee

- Brushing your teeth

- Unwinding with a nightly TV show

- Drinking a glass of wine with dinner

- Checking your phone in bed

These are perfect first dominoes to stack new habits onto!

Pick one of your routine triggers, then tack on your new habit right after it. For example:

- After morning coffee, meditate for 1 minute

- After brushing teeth, do 10 pushups

- After the TV show, read 1 chapter

- After wine, stretch for 5 minutes

When chained to an existing habit, your new behaviour inherits its automatic consistency! The engine is already running - just hop aboard.

Leverage old momentum to build new routines. Identify your non-negotiable habits and stack onto those.

Piggybacking works wonders. But you still gotta put in the work to design effective sequences. Experiment to find your perfect chains.

How marketing geniuses use the same tactic to trick your brain

The marketing gurus at KitKat were freakin' geniuses when they came up with their famous "Have a Break, Have a KitKat" slogan.

Those clever cats realised that office workers already had an ingrained habit of taking regular coffee breaks to recharge. This gave KitKat the perfect routine to piggyback onto!

The ads basically said: Yo office drones! When you take your hourly java refuelling break, chain on unwrapping our delicious wafer bars too.

KitKat becomes part of your sacred coffee routine - two habits linked! The cookie gets to coast on the already established momentum of the caffeine fix.

Brilliant right? Now every time someone pours a cup, their Pavlovian response is "Must...also...devour...chocolate..."

KitKat habituates the brain to associate their sugar rush with the coffee routine already locked in. Old habits fuels new ones. Two birds, one stone!

So take a page from KitKat's book. When looking to build new habits, scout out existing rituals you can seamlessly attach them to.

Leverage old momentum rather than starting from zero. Link habits cleverly like a candy bar piggybacking on coffee break nostalgia. You got this!

Build Your Habit Skyscraper Brick By Brick

Alright party people, when you meticulously design your habit sequences, it achieves something life-changing. Are you ready for this?...

You gradually construct the infrastructure that shapes your entire existence.

Boom! Let that sink in...

Your habits become the scaffolding and foundations that your lifestyle is built upon. The very blueprint for how your days unfold.

With proper planning, the cascades and stacks we map out transform our health, productivity, relationships, personal growth - you name it.

Each tiny habit is like laying another brick, slowly assembling your habit skyscraper. The effort is minimal, but the results add up to something massive.

Really take the time to thoughtfully arrange your habits for optimal chains. You are quite literally building your life one domino at a time baby!

Construct healthy habit infrastructure

Want to sculpt an incredible physique? Then methodically stack fitness micro-habits into your day.

Maybe it's:

- Morning mobility exercises

- 10 pushups after coffee

- Taking walks during lunch and mid-afternoon breaks

- Doing planks while dinner is in the oven

- Stretching during TV show commercial breaks

See how each flows into the next? With time, these habits build a bulletproof fitness fortress through incremental bricks.

Same idea for productivity infrastructure. Stack things like:

- Checking most important task first thing

- Powering through distractions to finish top priority

- Blocking time in calendar to plan next day

- Capture all random ideas into notebook even if just one sentence

- Reviewing calendar every Friday to optimise upcoming week

Again, one micro habit laid down after another creates the scaffolding. Your days become efficient machines.

You Must Become The Michelangelo of Habit Planning

Alright folks, listen up because this part is critical. I can't emphasise enough how key it is to become meticulous about planning your habit stacks.

Don't just casually slap some habits together and call it a day. Doing this half-assed is like building a house on a shoddy foundation - it will crumble fast.

To make these habit chains stick for the long haul, you need to be thoughtful about designing them. Become the Michelangelo of habit sequences - craft masterful cascades.

Put in the work upfront to analyse your lifestyle and experiment with different pairings. Learn your natural rhythms.

Find sequences that seamlessly fit into your daily flow. The triggers and transitions should click naturally, not feel forced.

For example, say you hate mornings and are groggy for hours after rolling out of bed. Don't try to stack intense exercise right after waking up.

Instead, put movement habits after your morning coffee, when you feel energised and motivated. Align it with your natural energy peaks for sustainability.

The more mindfully you test and craft these habit dominos, the more automatic your important routines become. Tiny changes flow effortlessly together into a better lifestyle.

It takes work, but designing these sequences is a game changer. You're slowly constructing the scaffolding for your destiny, brick by brick.

Imagine years from now looking back at the empire you built through steadily laying each habit foundation day after day. That's a legacy!

But it all starts with taking the time to become an artisan of habit planning. You got this. Now get designing!

If You Should Remember One Thing From This Chapter

Let's recap the key points about stackin' habits like Legos before moving on:

The name of the game is momentum - chain those small habits back-to-back to build routine cascades.

Plan sequences mindfully so each habit triggers the next automatically. Engineering the domino effect!

When habits build on each other in a logical flow, your productivity takes off. No friction or motivation needed!

Visualise setting up dominos - one habit knocks down the next. Feel the momentum build as each falls!

Use habit stacking for any area - health, work, learning, relationships, personal growth. Cascades work everywhere.

Be creative with your habit pairs based on your lifestyle. Morning tea > meditation > exercise is one example.

Also stack new habits onto old routines. Existing momentum is your friend! Add pushups after coffee, etc.

When you meticulously sequence habits, you build the infrastructure for an awesome lifestyle. Brick by brick!

Routine momentum achieved by design. Habit stacking takes your game to the next level once tiny habits are locked in.

But it only works through thoughtful planning and smart sequencing. Mindless habits scatter your energy.

Alright, now that we've got this habit cascade thing down, let's get social...

Leveraging accountability partners, groups and peer pressure sustains motivation as we'll see next. Let's go!

Chapter 3: Social Accountability - "Peer Pressure is Good: Harness the Power of Accountability Partners"

Friends, Grab Your Squad And Obliterate Those Goals

Trying to get shredded or write novels or learn languages solo is straight up masochism. It's just you versus your brain, and your brain is a hater.

Before long, you're bored, unmotivated, and scrolling Instagram instead of grinding habits. Not cool!

This is why we need to get social with it, folks. Surround yourself with hype beasts who lift you up, not bring you down. Let's leverage the power of squads for good!

Recruit Accountability Partners For A Power-Up Bonus

Alright folks, trying to implement big changes solo is like entering a boss battle without any potions or power-ups. Madness!

The smart move is to recruit accountability partners to join your quest. They provide that sweet sweet motivation and community boost!

Having even one accountability buddy is like unlocking a star power-up in Mario Kart. They keep you cruising down the habit highway at top speed with morale maxed out.

Here's why it works - knowing someone else is monitoring your progress means you CAN'T make excuses or lie to yourself. You'll feel obligated to crush workouts and stick to plans.

After all, you don't want to disappoint your gym pardner by slacking off! Letting down your team is the worst. So you grind 10x harder together than alone.

And when you share the habit building journey with others, succeeding becomes way more fun! Trying to PR your squat feels better when teammates are cheering you on.

Sharing the struggle builds way more camaraderie and motivation than solo training. We're social creatures by nature. Having a crew support you is game changing.

So consider making any habit you're trying to build more public. Share your goals on social media. Find online buddies. Talk about it.

And try to directly partner up with people close to you pursuing similar goals, like a workout buddy or writing partner. Keep each other on track!

Even just committing to one person helps - you'll subconsciously want to avoid disappointing them by giving up. That's the power of peer pressure and expectations!

Use it to your advantage. Surround yourself with hype men, motivators and allies. Make your habits open and social for that sweet accountability bonus!

Harness The Power Of World Wide Web Tribes And Habit Apps

Can't Find Local Friends Who Share Your Quirky Hobby? No Worries, The Online Tribe Has Your Back!

Listen, not everyone is blessed with an in-person friend group that shares your passion for underwater basket weaving or mediaeval sword fighting. And that's alright!

Thanks to the interwebz, you can now find like-minded weirdos who geek out about your niche interest from anywhere around the world. The online tribe is global, baby!

Seriously, for any hobby under the sun, there are forums, groups and apps to join. Share your sword fighting habit progress! Ask questions about basket weaving techniques!

Seeing posts from fellow sword-wielding, basket-crafting comrades provides camaraderie, inspiration, and accountability. You got this!

So even without local buddies, the worldwide web provides community to help you stick to your unconventional goals.

Let's explore some options...

Reddit For All Your Goals

Reddit is an amazing option for accountability and discussion around any goal or hobby under the sun. Seriously, it's scary and impressive.

There are subreddits for habits like fitness, meditation, writing, music and so much more. You'll find members at all levels sharing stories and tips.

Post your struggles staying consistent and folks will chime in with encouragement and strategies. Share your micro habit wins and people will celebrate your little victories.

Seeing posts from others on the same journey provides motivation and camaraderie. You can ask questions when stuck and trade habit hacks.

And if there isn't already a subreddit for your specific hobby, you can create one! Build the community you wish existed.

Fitness Apps For Virtual Training Buddies

For exercise habits, apps like Strava and Fitbit let you track runs, rides, workouts and more. You can join groups, follow friends and give each other kudos.

Knowing others will see your daily workout stats provides accountability to keep hitting your targets. You can even share training plans and nutrition tips.

It's amazing how motivating it can be to get a "Congrats!" from someone on the internet for your long run personal record. We crave social approval, even virtually!

Research confirms social fitness apps boost consistency and effort levels even without in-person interaction. So strap on your phone and go crush miles!

Financial Accountability With StickK

If you need even more extreme motivation, check out habit apps like StickK that let you put money on the line.

You can set financial stakes attached to your goals, like losing 5 dollars or publishing 5 articles. If you fail, the cash gets charged to you or donated.

You appoint an accountability referee to confirm if you hit the targets for the week. Missing them means penalty fees!

When your wallet is on the line, you're way more likely to stick to the habit. Fear of losing money is great motivation.

Online communities provide inspiration even when not in person. So tap into worldwide tribes! Just seeing others' progress can propel your own habits.

Seek Out Your People To Unleash Greatness

Alright folks, trying to achieve greatness solo gets old really fast. Pushing yourself with no one to share the journey with is DULL.

Sure, we all love a good underdog story about some lone hero. But in real life, lasting success depends a lot on community. As the African proverb goes: "If you want to go fast, go alone. If you want to go far, go together."

Let's take running for example. Trying to motivate yourself to solo slog miles everyday is ROUGH. Before long, you're skipping runs and making excuses.

But join a running crew, and suddenly you're pushing harder to keep up with the pack! You feel accountable to show up. Having folks expecting you makes it way more fun too.

It's why things like CrossFit boxes, cycling clubs, basketball teams and more are so popular. Working out alongside others provides community, competition and camaraderie that solitary training lacks.

Don't believe me? Just ask David Goggins, one of the world's toughest ultra endurance athletes. He swears his military background with intense team training led to his success.

We're social creatures wired to enjoy shared activity. Pursuing goals solo is needlessly hard mode. Don't try to muscle through alone. Seek out your people!

Find Your Tribe Through Clubs and Meetups

A great way to do this is look for clubs, classes or meetup groups around your existing hobbies or goals. That way there's a built-in community.

Like a running club if you want to stick to a running habit. A meditation centre if you're trying to meditate more. A writing group if you aspire to write. You get the idea.

Don't be shy about showing up alone and meeting fellow enthusiasts either. Most members are excited to welcome passionate newbies. Just take the leap!

Another option is forming Facebook Groups around specific goals like quitting smoking, reading more, or waking up early. Crowdsource accountability buddies.

Look online and offline. There are likely all sorts of communities already established around your goals. Find your niche tribe!

For added camaraderie, partner up directly with one or two friends who share your objectives. Check in regularly and cheer each other on.

Having just one consistent workout buddy or writing partner makes a massive difference. You feel more accountable when someone is expecting you to show up.

So reach out within those clubs and groups to find those ideal 1-2 accountability buddies. Your shared journey will be way more enjoyable and sustainable together.

Broadcast Your Journey To Hype Up Your Squad

You've assembled your accountability posse. Now it's time to let those hype beasts fully into your world!

Share the peaks and valleys of your habit journey with the group. This keeps everyone engaged to cheer you on.

Publicly post your goals, progress pics, habit stats, PRs, challenges, mini-wins...all of it. Celebrate milestones as a team.

Open up about the dream you're chasing and all the micro-steps along the way. Bring your community along on the ride.

When you share openly, your squad will feel more inspired to support you. They'll celebrate your habit PRs and help you troubleshoot setbacks.

Basically, loop your friends in on the real deal - wins, struggles, breakthroughs, everything. Bring your journey to life!

Doing this keeps you feeling motivated and accountable too. You won't wanna hide poor progress or shortcuts from your team.

So use any tools to share your quest - social media, group chats, vlogs, vision boards. However you do it, open up!

Let your hype crew see your commitment. Then watch them cheer you on louder than drunk sports parents as you level up!

Harness Social Media for Good

Platforms like Instagram and Facebook are perfect for this. Share your latest PR lift. Post weekly mileage charts. Flaunt habit streaks.

The endorphin rush of likes and comments is incredibly motivating. Positive reinforcement keeps you coming back.

And don't feel vain - it's not just fishing for compliments. You're putting your intentions out there to crystallise them. Public commitment effect baby!

Plus, knowing others are watching creates accountability to keep making progress. You'll work harder to avoid letting your peeps down.

So post those gym selfies and hold yourself to the fire! Vow to only share wins and milestones, not excuses. Social media karma inspired.

Celebrate Milestones as a Team

Beyond social platforms, mark habit milestones directly with your inner circle too. Party after you hit a big target!

Go out for dinner, share some champagne, exchange high fives. Make a ritual of celebrating key habits wins together.

Sharing the journey brings more joy to the grind. People invest more in goals when they feel part of the story. Let them own your success too!

Leverage your crew for some healthy competition as well. When you see friends scoring 'wins', it pushes you to step up.

Like if your buddy reads two books a month, you'll feel inspired to increase your reading volume and hit new PRs too.

Competing raises everyone's performance. Use it to motivate, not discourage. Habit PRs can be contagious!

So be open about your stats and progress. Let team members see your commitment and numbers. Harness those competitive juices for good.

Zuck Turns Annual Goals Into Social Media Gold

While we're on the topic of public accountability, we gotta talk about Mark Zuckerberg's savvy habit sharing strategy. That dude is next level with it!

At the start of each year, Zuck announces his personal goals and ambitions for the next 12 months. And we're talking big stuff - learn Mandarin, read 25 books, you know, casual resolutions.

But it doesn't stop there. Throughout the year, he gives frequent updates on his progress. Celebrates micro-wins and milestones. He shares lessons learned.

And his preferred medium for these habit journey updates? Yup, you guessed it - social media to his gazillion followers!

Zuck broadcasts his goals and accountability check-ins to the entire dang world. No privacy filters here, just straight up public journalling.

And you better believe the pressure of knowing millions are monitoring his goals keeps Zuck grinding hard to stick to the plans. He's publicly said that accountability helps him follow through.

It's social pressure and public commitment on steroids. Zuck can't fall off the habit wagon without looking bad when all eyes are on him.

He leverages the hype of his followers to stay motivated. And his frequent progress posts keep fanning the flames too. Well played sir!

Of course, being the CEO of the world's largest social network gives him a bit of an unfair advantage there. But the takeaway still applies.

Making your goals public and sharing the journey keeps you accountable. Let people track your progress and cheer you on!

So take a page from Zuckerberg's book. Tell the world what you're trying to accomplish this year and then chronicle the adventure.

Obviously you may not have billions of followers like Zuck does (jealous!). But share updates even if just for your inner circle. They want to support you!

If You Should Remember One Thing From This Chapter

Let's recap the need-to-know stuff about getting social with habits:

Trying to grind solo is madness - we need squads to keep us motivated and honest.

Find an accountability partner to boost your habits. Make it public to create mutual expectations.

Online communities provide remote camaraderie and inspiration too. Use Reddit, apps, groups.

Research confirms social pressure improves consistency even virtually. Find your people.

Join clubs and meetups around your hobbies and goals for built-in community.

Have training partners and share your habit journey for accountability and fun competition.

Use streak posts and progress pics to keep each other pumped. Positive hype!

As habits get contagious in your squad, you end up motivating each other. Rising tides lift all boats!

Bottom line - stop trying to solo carry the world. We need companionship and peer pressure.

Surround yourself with allies sharing the journey. Thrive together.

Alright, now that we've got the power of the posse down, let's talk about the real black magic - compound interest! This is the game changer...

Chapter 4: Compound Success - The compound effect of disciplined habits over time

Friends, Tiny Steps Create Massive Change...Eventually

Alright folks, time to talk about the big daddy habit secret: compound interest!

Not as sexy as it sounds - we're not getting into money market accounts. But applied to habits, compounding is an absolute game changer.

Stick with micro habits long enough, and the results grow exponentially over time. We're talking sneaky ninja level change.

It's like a snowball effect...you start small, but gathering momentum rolls that snowball into a giant boulder crashing down the mountain. Tiny turns to titanic.

Let's break it down...

Compounding 101

Remember compound interest from maths class? Boring concept, but crazy powerful over time.

You invest just $100 bucks a month at 10% annual return. After a decade, it's grown to $19,000. Twenty five years, $118,000. Forty seven years, over $1 million!

Websites grow the same way. Keep writing consistently for years, and your small blog attracts more readers and income over time.

The key is consistency. You must steadily add effort without long breaks, or else progress resets to zero. Skipping days destroys compounding.

How Habits Compounds

Let's break it down...

Same as compound interest - you steadily contribute small amounts, and the growth accelerates exponentially. Before you know it, you've got a fat bank account.

But how does this apply to habits? Excellent question, dear lazy reader!

The mechanics are the same - small consistent actions stack up way quicker than you expect. Take pushups for example.

One lousy pushup requires virtually zero effort. But do just that single rep every day for a year straight, and you'll have done 365 pushups without noticing!

But imagine you steadily grow the number of pushups you do every month by 20%

After 5 years of that daily habit, you'll have completed 1,more than 10 thousand pushups. That's 100x more than you imagined when you started.

The reps seem trivial day by day. But the output compounds dramatically over time thanks to unrelenting consistency. Pushups start to add up fast!

It's the same story with meditation. One measly minute doesn't seem like much on its own.

But stick with that micro-habit each day, grow it steadily and after a decade you'll have meditated for over thousands of hours! One minute became thousands of hours. Tell me that's not crazy!

Again, it's easy to underestimate how even tiny habits pay off in the long run through compounding gains.

Any habit works this way - reading, writing, journaling, learning guitar. Small strides made routinely stack up the results big time.

But, and this is key, you absolutely gotta put in the reps daily for the compound gains to work their magic.

Skipping days constantly resets progress to zero. You must feed the bird each day without fail. Consistency above all.

That's why most people don't see results from habits - they expect big changes immediately. When they still don't have a six pack after one week of pushups, they quit.

But true transformation happens through months and years of micro habits compounding incrementally in the background. The results eventually astonish but you gotta stick it out.

It's like slowly accumulating compound interest in a bank account - the exponential growth isn't obvious at first. But after years of deposits, suddenly you've got a fortune.

So be patient with your habits! Embrace the gradual compounding gains. Remember the wise saying - "inch by inch, life's a cinch; yard by yard, life is hard." Take it inch by inch!

Micro-optimize Your Habits Through Marginal Gains

We've covered how small consistent actions compound into huge results over time. Now let's dial that in even more using something athletes call marginal gains.

This one simple trick can massively boost your habit results. The gist is to micro-optimize every tiny detail related to your routine.

Elite athletes are masters at this. They obsessively tweak nutrition, sleep, form, equipment, recovery, mental prep and more.

No single optimization makes a big difference alone. But together, those 1% improvements create massive advantages.

Take pro cyclists for example. They may meticulously adjust:

- Bike seat angle by half a degree

- Test countless aerodynamic helmet designs

- Try various energy gel brands for fueling

- Dial in nutrition and hydration needs

- Vary training locations and techniques

- Refine recovery stretches and foam rolling

Individually, these changes are meaningless. But over time, they compound into huge race results and podium finishes. Tiny gains become massive through marginal gains.

This works for any habit. Think about how you can improve every aspect just 1%:

With exercise - add one rep, perfect your form, focus on breathing, recovery stretches, protein intake. Tweak it all!

Meditation - extend it one minute, refine posture, try different music, switch up location. Micro-optimize!

Writing - change locations to inspire creativity, use apps to eliminate distractions, experiment with different pens. Identify and improve small factors.

When you track and tune all these granular details, your habit routine levels up exponentially. It all stacks up!

Be 1% Better Every Day

Strive to get 1% better at your habits each day in small ways:

- One extra push up

- Perfect meditation posture -Eliminate one distraction

- Wake up 15 minutes earlier

These micro-wins compound rapidly. Before you know it, your habits are radically improved through relentless 1% progress.

So take inspiration from elite athletes and their compulsive micromanaging. Sweat the small stuff! Tiny optimizations eventually create massive results.

Slow And Steady Habits Win The Race Through Tortoise Mentality

When it comes to habits, slow and steady consistency will always beat intense sprints followed by burning out. We gotta channel that wise old tortoise mentality.

It's easy to get over eager and try to go full hare mode out the gates. You intensely diet or train fueled by motivation, determined that this time will be different!

But let's be real - that ambitious intensity never lasts. After a week or two, you're fried and ready to throw in the towel. Going hard and fast backfires.

The tortoise knows better. He takes it slowly with calm, steady determination. Tiny incremental progress day after day.

It may seem painfully slow at first, inching towards the finish line. But the tortoise eventually gets there through disciplined consistency.

Apply this to your habits. Don't fixate on rapid transformation or big numbers immediately. Take it inch by inch with micro habits practised daily.

So pace yourself for the long game. Be 1% better through achievable micro habits vs intense bursts. Progress will steadily accumulate.

Establish the discipline and patience mindset to sustain habits over the years. Compounding works its magic in the background if you just stick with it!

Trust The Process - Stick With It Even When You Don't See Results

Alright folks, this is one of the hardest but most critical mindset shifts for habits to click: Trusting the process.

Sometimes you can diligently stick to your micro habits, yet still not see obvious progress after a month or two. This is normal! Remain patient and keep the faith.

It takes time for tiny gains to compound dramatically. But they are accruing in the background even when it seems invisible day to day.

Your effort is silently stacking up - those micro habit reps are laying the foundation. Even if you don't notice changes yet, neural pathways are getting wired.

Consistency now is setting the stage for massive results later. But you gotta trust the process. Don't get discouraged by invisible progress early on.

For example, maybe you've meditated 1 minute everyday for a month. Easy right? But you still feel stressed and scattered.

Doesn't seem like it's "working" yet! But hold the course. After a year, suddenly you'll realise you carved out hours of mindfulness. Just stick with it!

Or doing one pushup a day - seems pointless at first. But hang in there, and after months you'll be shocked by the strength you've built through sheer consistency.

The compounding effect takes time to visibly materialise. But micro habits today compound into unbelievable achievements over the long run.

So keep grinding out those tiny routines even when progress appears non-existent. Have faith in the process! The results will blow your mind soon enough.

Just stay the course with tiny consistency. Your micro efforts are silently getting you ready for greatness. Trust the process - one baby step at a time!

Jerry Seinfeld Cracked The Comedy Game Through Micro Habits

When it comes to comedy royalty, Jerry Seinfeld reigns supreme. So how did Mr. Bee Movie reach the pinnacle of comedic greatness? You guessed it - tiny habits baby!

See, most newbie stand ups try the rapid rise strategy - book the biggest clubs, create an hour special ASAP, pray to get discovered quickly.

And they flame out even faster. Comedy takes craft, and craft takes habits. Jerry knew this.

While others scrambled for overnight fame, Jerry focused on honing his material at crappy open mics night after night. He ruthlessly rehearsed the basics.

He took baby steps - 5 minutes here, 10 minutes there. Jerry chopped each joke down to perfection. He tweaked and tightened relentlessly.

Other comics regarded Jerry's style as too goofy and mundane. "Who wants jokes about cereal and airline food?" they scoffed.

But Jerry understood what we've been preaching in this book - teeny tiny gains compound!

With enough reps, those mundane observations became devastatingly incisive cultural commentary. Jerry burned the basic principles into his brain through habit.

In fact, legend has it that early on Jerry would write new jokes and rehearse them on stage up to 200 times until they were bulletproof.

Two. Hundred. Times. That's how you develop mastery! Practise the micro habits and small wins again and again.

Jerry focused on polishing his skills, not chasing fame. After 12 years of honing his style at small comedy clubs, seemingly overnight he became a sensation.

But as we know, that success was built on a foundation of hundreds of micro habits and jokes iterated to perfection.

Pretty soon Jerry was booking stadium shows and filming his legendary sitcom about the inane minutiae of life. All because he started small and practised habits constantly.

So What Habits Powered Seinfeld's Success?

Jerry optimised his entire lifestyle for comedy gains:

- He wrote jokes daily to generate constant new material

- He tested jokes at clubs nightly to refine timing and delivery

- He surrounded himself with funny friends to exchange ideas

- He travelled the country doing gigs to build real world experience

- He observed mundane life for joke ideas and wrote them in tiny notebooks

- He lived lean early on so he could focus purely on comedy, not cash

- It was never about grand gestures or overnight success for Jerry. His habits focused on incremental daily gains - writing one joke, testing one bit, honing his craftsmanship.

This allowed Jerry to not just achieve success, but sustain it for decades as the GOAT. Consistency always wins the long game.

If You Should Remember One Thing From This Chapter

Let's recap the key lessons about the power of compound interest for habits:

Compounding works like a snowball effect - start small, gather momentum over time. Killer results ahead!

The key is unrelenting consistency. Don't skip days or else progress resets to zero.

Skipping destroys the compounding cycle. You must feed the bird daily for magic.

When applied to habits, tiny efforts stack up results shockingly fast through compounding.

With patience, those micro habits transform your body and skills before you know it. But you gotta believe in the process.

Have faith when you don't see obvious results after a month. Your effort is silently stacking...impact takes time.

Think marginal gains too - tiny optimizations compound into huge advantages over the long run.

Compounding requires a tortoise mentality. Slow and steady habits outrun short bursts.

Trust the process and have faith. Your micro habits today compound into remarkable results tomorrow!

Alright, we've covered the 4 key ingredients - tiny habits, stacking, social pressure, compounding. Now it's time to put these all together...

Next up, we'll explore how to combine these elements into an integrated system. Let's do this!

Chapter 5: The system - Putting it all together

Alright Friends, Time To Combine These Powers Like Voltron!

We've covered the 4 ingredient secret formula for transforming your life with minimum effort. Now let's look at how to integrate these elements into one seamless, Voltron-like mega-robot of productivity!

Individually, tiny habits, stacking, social pressure and compounding are all powerful. But together they form an unstoppable system for steering your lifestyle to greatness through micro-actions.

Let me paint you a picture...

The Setup

First, you start tiny. I'm talking embarrassingly tiny habits - one pushup, one minute reading, one sentence journaled.

These micro-changes are laughably easy to stay consistent with day after day. And they steadily build momentum.

Next, you sequence these mini habits for cascades. After your morning coffee, knock out those pushups. After pushups, meditate for a minute. After meditating, read one page. See the momentum build?

To take it up a notch, tell your friends! Share your tiny habit goals on social media. Join online groups. Light that fire under your butt through accountability.

Now the magic...just keep those mini habits up every single day, no matter how small they seem. Because they will compound into shocking results over time, guaranteed.

How It All Comes Together

When done right, these elements combine into a system running on autopilot. Here's how it looks:

The tiny habits phase lowers resistance so consistency is easy. You don't procrastinate on one pushup or minute reading! And micro-wins motivate faster than big goals.

Habit stacking develops cascades that remove friction and decision-making. Your sequenced routines flow one into the next without thought.

Social pressure keeps you honest through accountability. You can't quit when peers are watching and cheering you on! Competition and community develop.

And compounding works behind the scenes. Those tiny habits stack up results and transform your life stealthily over weeks, months and years.

Before you know it, you've tricked your brain into building killer habits, just by nudging yourself 1% more in the right direction each day.

It takes some thoughtful planning, but the system runs on autopilot once designed well. It becomes an effortless Voltron-like assembly of tiny habits transforming your entire lifestyle.

Build The System For Your Life

Obviously, this exact formula won't work for everyone. We each need a unique system tailored to our goals and personality.

But use this as your blueprint - start micro, stack habits, get accountability partners, trust the compounding process.

Reflect on your own lifestyle and needs, then engineer your system accordingly. Test different sequences and accountable partnerships until you find the groove.

It may take some trial and error, but once you nail the formula, it's like a magical roadmap to self-improvement through micro steps.

Don't underestimate the power of small consistent actions. They seem trivial at first, but practice pays exponential dividends over time.

Plant those seeds through tiny habits + smart sequencing + social pressure + compounding = you'll grow into the most awesome version of yourself before you know it!

Alright team, that concludes our habit-hacking adventure! Now go take action and start gradually steering your life where you want it to go.

You got this. Be patient, trust the process, and believe in the compounded micro-changes you're making daily.

I'll leave you with this final thought from the great philosopher Julia A. Carney: "Little drops of water, Little grains of sand, Make the mighty ocean And the beauteous land."

You're already building your mountain, one brick at a time. Keep stacking my friends!

Conclusion

Friends, We Did It! Now Go Crush Life With Your New Superpowers

Well hot damn folks, we finally made it to the end of this wild habit-hacking rollercoaster ride! It's been quite the journey - like an R-rated Pixar movie filled with potty language and zero safety harnesses.

But we survived! And now you're armed with all the sneakily simple secrets for upgrading your life without bogus willpower. Well done champ! Seriously, massive props.

Give yourself a hearty pat on the back. Or even better - bust out one celebratory pushup for crushing this book! Then call up your mom to tell her you finally finished a self-help book. She'll be so proud she may even send you $20 in the mail!

For real though - take a moment to let your achievement fully sink in. Reading these game-changing concepts was the easy part. Now the real work begins in actually applying these habit hacks.

But if you take action, your life will transform so fast it'll make your head spin like that freaky demon child from The Exorcist. In a year you'll be the productivity master that friends beg for advice.

So get out there and win at life! Build those micro habits. Surround yourself with hype beasts. Have faith in the process. And prove the haters and your own self-doubts wrong.

I believe in you guys 100%! We may be total strangers, but reading this book proves you already have the hunger and curiosity it takes to level up. Now it's time to claim the awesome life you deserve.

Allow yourself to vividly envision and get excited about the incredible future self these habits will build. Let that vision pull you forward each day.

That disciplined, fulfilled, thriving person you dream of becoming is counting on you to put in the work. One tiny habit at a time, you're unlocking your true potential. How freakin' cool is that?

Alright, enough sappiness. Go forth and dominate! This is your time to shine homie. Power up and kick some booty! You were born for this.

I'm wishing you an epic journey filled with compounding gains, seamless habit momentum, socially fueled motivation, and 1% daily progress. You've so freakin' got this!

As for me, I'm off to go practice what I preach. Gotta knock out these micro habits...one teensy step at a time towards my own big hairy audacious goals.

But for real - from the bottom of my heart, thanks for taking this habit-change adventure with me.

Alright, enough sappiness. Go dominate! This is your time.

Now if you'll excuse me, I've got some tiny habits to practise...one push-up at a time.

Keep hustlin' friends! Until we meet again.

Why I Had To Share The Habit Hacks That Changed My Life

Alright folks, before we part ways, let's get real for a minute. It's time to peel back the curtain on what inspired me to write this wacky habit hacking manifesto in the first place.

Let me share the origin story of what inspired this book in the first place. It all started a few years back when I noticed some friends struggling. And I don't mean "struggling" in a dramatic way, just feeling kinda stuck.

See, on the surface these folks had it all - sweet jobs, relationships, toys and vacations. They projected an image of success.

But behind the scenes, they battled lack of motivation, stress, and feeling adrift. I realised even "successful" peeps felt like frauds.

Meanwhile, I was oddly content. I had energy, direction, and solid routines. Definitely no yacht though! Soon maybe...

What was my secret? The habit hacks we've covered here! Tiny changes created massive results over time.

Friends said achieving their dreams seemed impossible. But I knew small consistent actions could get them there.

So I wrote a mini habit guide to share with my inner circle. They needed help and tough love.

I laid out the key tactics - start micro, build momentum, get accountable. I explained how tiny steps compound.

And it worked! Friends' mindsets and lifestyles transformed within months of applying the strategies.

One buddy Jose used to stay up till 3am doom scrolling but then optimised his sleep, diet and focus through micro habits. Soon he got promoted twice at work.

Another friend Sofia never thought she could stick to a diet. But tiny nutrition swaps and peer accountability helped her drop 40 lbs steadily.

Once I saw the impact, I realised I had to create a proper book elaborating on these habit hacks that changed my life, and share it with the world.

With this book, I want to make habit change accessible for regular folks who don't relate to intense guru advice.

Just start small and be patient. Consistency pays off. I'm here to keep you motivated and laughing!

Okay, enough sincerity. Let's crush life! I believe in you guys. Go show me what you're made of ;)

You Need More Habit Knowledge In Your Life! Peep These Epic Reads

I know some of you beasts will finish this book jonesing for more of that sweet, sweet habit info. No judgement! Learning is addictive.

Lucky for you, I've got a master list of the most epic habit hack books out there to further your nerdery. Get hype!

1) "Atomic Habits" by James Clear

This is the undisputed bible for all things habit related. James Clear breaks down the psychology and neuroscience behind how to actually build habits that stick.

You'll learn how to hack your habit loops, how tiny changes compound into results, and practical strategies to implement this in your life. It's like getting a PhD in habit mechanics!

The book goes deep but explains things in a simple way - none of that convoluted academese. And it's packed with engaging real-world examples of how these tactics work for athletes, companies, and more.

If you read just one more habit book (but let's be real, you know you won't) make it this one!

2) "The Power of Habit" by Charles Duhigg

An OG classic! Duhigg explores why our habits exist and how they drive 40% of our daily choices. Sometimes we're just lizards without a brain following programmed sequences without realising it.

But the great news is you CAN reprogram your habitual thinking patterns by hacking the habit loop. Duhigg breaks down how to identify and change your triggers, routines, and rewards.

This book will enlighten you with science-backed insight on human behaviour. But don't worry, it's not dry at all. Duhigg packs it with fascinating case studies from real organisations making habit shifts.

By the end, you'll be buzzing with ideas on how to overhaul your habits for success. Just try not to freak people out by analyzing all their unconscious tics!

3) "Hooked" by Nir Eyal

Alright, don't judge me too harshly for recommending this one! Yes, it's a guide for designing habit-forming products and services to get people addictively hooked.

But it's also super fascinating to understand exactly how tech companies covertly build "sticky" user habits with reward loops and variable reinforcement.

Once you know their tricks, you can avoid getting sucked into unhealthy habits yourself. And you may pick up some persuasive psychology tactics to apply in your own life ;)

4) "Habit Stacking" by S.J. Scott

S.J. Scott is like the MacGyver of habit hacking. He creatively combines small changes to stack into significant lifestyle upgrades.

The book provides 97 micro habit ideas you can mix and match. Like eat one vegetable daily. Talk to one stranger daily. Walk 100 steps after each meal. Tiny shifts that pair well together.

Scott keeps things simple while teaching you how to design optimized cascades. You'll learn to chain together physical, mental, emotional and social micro habits for maximum results.

Basically, this book removes any excuse that changes must be big and overwhelming. You got this!

5) "Tiny Habits" by B.J. Fogg

The OG pioneer of the "start tiny" philosophy! B.J. Fogg's work at Stanford revealed how you can build habits through small steps - as long as you nail the timing and triggers.

He developed the Tiny Habits® method which is genius in its simplicity. Just attaching new habits to an existing daily behaviour makes them stick.

Like doing squats after hanging up your coat when you get home. Fogg's book will illuminate how tiny is the path of least resistance when trying to create or disrupt routines.

You'll learn to appreciate the power of small things. After reading, you'll never overlook tiny ants colonising your kitchen again!

6) "Switch" by Chip & Dan Heath

If reading this habit book sparked your personal revolution, Switch is the perfect sequel. It dives deep into actually making change stick when life is crazy.

The Heath brothers are experts at making science engaging. They break down how to direct your mental "rider", motivate your emotional "elephant", and shape your environment for success.

This book provides awesome insights into overcoming inertia, managing emotions, and creating new neural pathways. It's like Inside Out meets Inception - a mind trip for tricking yourself into positive change.

Pretty soon you'll be nudging your routine onto autopilot by hacking your psyche. Take that lazy brain!

7) "The Compound Effect" by Darren Hardy

Alright, time for some tough love. This book from success guru Darren Hardy will call you out for looking for quick fixes rather than compound gains. Ouch...

But that's what we need sometimes! Hardy provides example after example of how small, boring habits create massive results over decades.

You'll learn how eating an apple daily can make you lose 100+ lbs. How reading just 30 pages a day can make you an expert. How pennies and nickels can grow into millions.

Basically, this will hammer home everything we talked about with consistency, incremental gains, and not expecting overnight success. You got this, but it takes time and micro habits!

8) "Better Than Before" by Gretchen Rubin

Gretchen Rubin is like a habit scientist studying herself. She relentlessly tested different self-improvement theories on herself to see what actually works in real life.

The result is an incredible framework on how we can hack our patterns to be more productive, creative, healthy and happy.

You'll learn tactics based on whether you're an abstainer, moderator or rebel when it comes to habits. And how to create accountability, cue rituals, manage procrastination and more based on your style.

Rubin keeps it relatable and actionable with stories from test driving the strategies on her own life first. Get ready for a habit rollercoaster ride!

9) "Mindset" by Carol Dweck

Before we can even talk about transforming your habits, Mindset argues you need to upgrade your core belief system. Are you fixed or growth oriented?

Dweck explains how adopting a growth mindset, where you believe you can improve, is key to unlocking your potential. It creates the mental framework for sustaining habit change.

This book will get you fired up through research and stories about people utilising the growth approach to achieve greatness in sports, business, academics and beyond.

It may not feel directly applicable at first, but mindset is the foundation that gives your habits room to flourish. Read this!

10) "Willpower" by Roy Baumeister

Last but not least, recharge your willpower reserves with this science-backed book on self-control. You can only resist so many cookies and Insta pings before ego depletion!

But by better understanding how willpower works as a limited daily resource, you can optimise and harness it for habits.

You'll learn how to feed willpower, reduce decision fatigue, leverage peer pressure, and make the most of your mental energy. Think of it like an athlete training the muscle of self-discipline.

You Need A Way To Track Your Habit Use This Simple Template

Wanna go to the next level with your habit game? Whip out your pen and craft table, it's time to build a habit tracker, baby!

This bad boy allows you to meticulously document your progress like a scientist observing a rare mating ritual.

First up, lay out your column headings across the top - all 7 days of the week from Sunday funday to Saturday shindig.

Then down the left side, write out the specific habits you want to track - like doing 10 pushups or sticking to your Paleo diet or avoid rage spiralling on Twitter.

This creates neatly organised boxes for each habit/day combo. Now here's the fun part -

Everyday, fill in the boxes to record whether you completed each habit or failed spectacularly. Checkmark for success, X for failure!

Your table becomes a data map of adherence and backsliding. Revel in your tiny habit triumphs, analyse the screw ups.

This tracker allows you to spot patterns too. Maybe you unravel on Mondays and Fridays. Time to rally the social accountability squad!

So bust out your pens, embrace your inner cartographer. Meticulously document your habit journey - the victories, the failures, all of it!

Calling All Book Nerds - Your Mission, Should You Choose To Accept It...

Welcome, fellow habit hacker! Now that you've joined me on this wacky self-improvement odyssey, I have just one small favour to request.

In the spirit of paying-it-forward, it would be mega dope if you could take a sec to leave an honest positive review about your experience with this book. I know, I know - just hear me out!

See, your feedback has more power than you realise. Taking 1 minute to share your positive thoughts provides a massive solid.

Positive reviews give the mystical book algorithms signals that these habit tips are truly helping real humans upgrade their lives (aka you!).

This then gives the book more visibility so others can also benefit from the knowledge. Your review spreads the love.

And your unique perspective may give future readers that final nudge of inspiration to take action. Like a recommendation from a trusted friend, you feel?

Especially for a funky little indie book like this, reviews help enormously. So if it resonated and brought value, please boost the signal!

The goal is getting these habit hacks in front of as many people as possible. Your review fuels the flywheel.

So sincerely, thank you for even considering.

Onward and upward, friends.